NOT BECOMING MY MOTHER

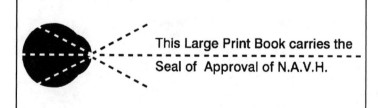

This Large Print Book carries the
Seal of Approval of N.A.V.H.

NOT BECOMING
MY MOTHER
AND OTHER THINGS
SHE TAUGHT ME
ALONG THE WAY

RUTH REICHL

THORNDIKE PRESS
A part of Gale, Cengage Learning

GALE
CENGAGE Learning

Detroit • New York • San Francisco • New Haven, Conn • Waterville, Maine • London

GALE
CENGAGE Learning™

Copyright © Ruth Reichl, 2009.
Thorndike Press, a part of Gale, Cengage Learning.

ALL RIGHTS RESERVED
Thorndike Press® Large Print Biography.
The text of this Large Print edition is unabridged.
Other aspects of the book may vary from the original edition.
Set in 18 pt. Plantin.
Printed on permanent paper.

LIBRARY OF CONGRESS CATALOGING-IN-PUBLICATION DATA

Reichl, Ruth.
    Not becoming my mother : and other things she taught me
along the way / by Ruth Reichl.
        p. cm.
    Originally published: New York : Penguin Press, 2009.
    ISBN-13: 978-1-4104-1573-8 (lg. print. : hardcover : alk.
paper)
    ISBN-10: 1-4104-1573-2 (lg. print. : hardcover : alk. paper)
    1. Reichl, Ruth. 2. Reichl, Miriam. 3. Women food writers—
United States—Biography. 4. Large type books. I. Title.
TX649.R45A3 2009b
641.5092--dc22
[B]   2009004940

Published in 2009 by arrangement with The Penguin Press, a member
of Penguin Group (USA) Inc.

Printed in the United States of America
1 2 3 4 5 6 7 13 12 11 10 09

For you, Mom. Finally.

CONTENTS

THE MIM TALES

My mother's name was Miriam, but most people called her Mim. She was such a character that as a child I developed a special form of literature; it was known as the Mim Tale. This is one of my favorites.

"Hurry up, hurry up," my mother is shouting as she races through our small apartment, "we're going to be late again!"

This is nothing new; my mother is incapable of arriving anywhere on time. But she has just become the leader of my Brownie troop, and the powers that be have emphasized the importance of punctuality. She grabs a red hat, crams it onto her head, and dashes for the door. I am right behind her. Just as the door begins to close Mom shouts, "Oh, no, I forgot the snack!"

"Mom," I moan. "You can't forget the snack again. You forgot it last week."

"Don't be fresh!" she snaps, inserting herself into the arc of the closing door. "We have no time to shop. Come back in and help me find something delicious."

"We don't have anything," I say flatly.

"Nonsense," she says, striding to the refrigerator. She surveys the contents with a gimlet eye and gingerly extracts a bowl. It is covered with bright blue fuzz, but she care-fully scrapes this off, murmuring, "This must be that chocolate pud-ding I made last month." She pokes in a finger, tastes tentatively and says triumphantly, "What a good start!"

"There's not very much," I say hopefully. I am aware that any men-tion of the pudding's antique charac-ter will be unwelcome; my mother is a firm believer in the benign nature of mold. "It's not enough for all of us."

"I know that!" she says crossly. "We're going to stretch it. See what you can find in the cupboard."

"Like what?" I ask dubiously.

"Oh, use your imagination," she snaps.

I climb onto the stove so I can reach the cupboard, give the door, which sticks a bit, a firm yank and peer inside. I pull out a box of pretzels, a few prunes, a bag of very stale marshmallows and a jar of strawberry jam. "Perfect!" says Mom. "Hand them down here. Anything else?"

Feeling it would be unwise to mention the sardines or the tin of liver pâté, I pass on to the can of peaches. "Good," says Mom, "give me that too."

As I watch, Mom mixes the jam into the not very moldy chocolate pudding and adds the prunes. "Break those pretzels into little pieces," she commands, "while I chop up the marshmallows and slice the peaches. This is going to be delicious!"

Three minutes later she is wiping her hands. "Let's go," she says.

"Aren't you taking plates?" I ask.

"We can't just use our fingers."

Mom sticks a dozen soupspoons in her pocket and cries merrily, "The girls will think it's such fun to eat right out of the bowl!"

I am dubious about this, but to my surprise, they do. While my best friend, Jeanie, and I stick our spoons ostentatiously in and out, consuming nothing, the rest of the girls happily gobble up the goop. "Mrs. Reichl," says Nancy Feld, a dreadful little toady of a child, "you're such a wonderful cook. Could you give the recipe to my mother?"

Mom rewards her with a queenly smile. "Call me Mim, dear," she says, "but I couldn't do that; the recipe is an old family secret." And then she turns to me and whispers triumphantly, "See, I told you. A little mold never hurt anyone!"

I've got Mim Tales by the dozen, and I've used them for years to entertain my friends. As a writer I've always known how lucky I was to have so much material, and my first book opened with Mom accidentally poisoning a couple of dozen people at a party. After the book was published people kept asking, "Did she really do those things?"

She did. But that doesn't mean she wanted the world to know about it. Telling stories to your friends is one thing, but a book is quite another, and I would never have written it while she was still alive. Although I omitted the most embarrassing tales, the first time I held the printed book in my hands I winced. I could not keep from thinking that I had betrayed my mother. It was not a good feeling, and I wanted to make it up to her.

I knew that there was a box filled with Mom's diaries and letters, and I was determined to try and find it. She had always wanted to write a book about her life, and I thought that I should do it for her. I owed her that much.

But when I couldn't find the box I dropped the project, going on to write a second memoir, and then a third, each time getting deeper into my mother's debt. Some day, I kept saying, I'll write Mom's book.

Then last year, on what would have been her hundredth birthday, I sat down to write one of those speeches in which people traditionally thank their mothers. I scribbled words unthinkingly, but when I looked down at the page I found that I had written something like a Mim Tale. But this was in a different voice, more hers than mine, and it was finally telling her side of the story.

"My mother would have been one hundred years old today," the speech began. "And so I've been thinking about her, and how she helped me to become the person that I am."

She did not do it any of the ordinary ways. She was not a great writer, or a great businesswoman, or even, if truth be told, a particularly good mother. I think she tried to be a good wife, but she wasn't much at keeping house, and I don't think I've ever met anyone who was a worse cook.

But my mother was a great example of everything I didn't want to be, and to this day I wake up every morning grateful that I'm not her. Grateful, in fact, not to be any of the women of her generation, who were unlucky enough to have been born at what seems to me to have been the worst possible time to have been a middle-class American woman.

When my mother was five she answered the telephone by saying this: "How often are the pains coming?" Little wonder, then, that she wanted to go to medical school and become a doctor like her father. But when she announced this to her parents they looked her up and down and said, "You're no beauty, and it's too bad that you're such an intellectual. But if you become a doctor no man will ever marry you." So Mom got a PhD in musicology. The family was musical; her mother would later become an impresario, the Sol Hurok of Cleveland.

My grandmother was, by everybody's estimation, a formidable businesswoman. She brought great musicians to Cleveland, she started a lecture series, and Mom said she could look at any theater and count the house in a second. But when the hard times ended, my grandmother folded her business. As she later explained, her work was just a stop-gap measure, her way of helping out when money was scarce. Good women didn't work if they didn't have to; it would only humiliate their husbands and make the world think their men were incapable of supporting them.

So Mom took her degree and opened a bookshop; it was a ladylike profession, and although it was not the medical career that she had yearned for, it made her happy. She did marry, but not until she was almost thirty, late enough that the word "spinster" was being whispered behind her back. And sure enough, after the wedding everyone expected her to settle down, leave her shop behind and have babies.

There were a few problems with this plan. In the first place, Mom wasn't exactly maternal; babies bored her to tears. Happily, in her time there were nursemaids to care for the kids; I'll bet my mother never changed a diaper. And that is precisely the problem; she didn't do much else either. In earlier times keeping house had been a full-time job, even for those with servants, but by the time Mom married so many labor-saving devices had been introduced that cooking and cleaning just didn't take that long. My mother, like most of her friends, literally had nothing to do.

I have never known so many

unhappy people. They were smart, they were educated and they were bored. Some of them did charitable work, but it wasn't fulfilling. Their misery was an ugly thing, and it was hard on their families. It was a terrible waste of talent and energy, and watching them I knew that I was never going to be like them.

Every night, when my father came in from work, he'd set his briefcase down in the hall, and I saw the little transformation that occurred. I realized that his secret life, the one he had when he was away from us, nurtured him, fed his soul. I watched him leaving in the morning, wishing that my mother could go to work too. I thought if she had her own secret life she would be a happier person. And I determined, when I was very small, that no matter what, nobody was going to keep me from having a work life. I thought then — and I still think now — that it is the key to happiness.

And so today, when people ask, "Why do you work so hard?" I think of my mother, who was not allowed to do it, and say, "Because I can."

This was not a Mim Tale, but Mom's story had struck a nerve and over the next few weeks I began getting letters from people I did not know. They all began the same way: "My mother was just like yours . . ."

The letters kept on coming and several people suggested that I write a book about Mom's generation. The idea intrigued me, and I began interviewing other women, taking notes about their mothers and their thwarted lives.

But when the time came to start writing, I found I couldn't. For months I sat staring at the notes with absolutely no idea of where to begin. I went to the library and perused old newspapers. I read the Nineteenth Amendment to the Constitution and tried to imagine what it must have been like, belonging to that first generation of women who had been granted equal rights. I studied the work of suffragettes. But each time I tried to write about emancipated women I found myself going in circles, uncertain of what to say.

Why did it take me so long to figure out that I had been handed the perfect opportunity to write my mother's book? Only later did I understand how frightened I had been, how scared of what I might find out.

Like most women, I decided who my mother was long ago, sometime during childhood. The comic character of the Mim Tales was safe now; I had spent many years making peace with her. Her voice was no longer inside my head and it was a relief to have all that behind me. I was reluctant to replace the mother I thought I knew with someone else. Why go looking for trouble?

But I owed it to my mother, and I knew it. Still, every time I headed toward the basement where the box of diaries might be I turned away, experiencing an urgent need to bake a pie, run an errand, wax the floors.

In the end I managed to persuade myself that the box was very likely to be lost. That gave me the courage to finally open up the basement door and creep slowly down the chilly stairs.

Feeling like Pandora, I picked my way through outgrown skis, discarded tools, old menus and ancient type-writers, peering into the dusty car-tons that towered over me. The one containing Mom's notes was nowhere to be found, and I was beginning to breathe easy when I stumbled over a once-shiny white box held together with pieces of twine. Blowing off the dirt, I read "Miriam's Life and Let-ters" penciled in my father's calligraphic script, the writing almost obliterating the stamped B. Altman & Co. beneath it.

The top crumbled in my hand — it had been years since anyone had touched it — and opened to reveal a huge collection of letters, notes and clippings. Looking down I caught sight of my mother's bold handwriting and inhaled sharply. It was as if she were suddenly with me, there in the basement, and as I bent to pick up a sheet of paper covered with her vivid scrawl I could almost hear her voice. I sat down on the cold cement floor and let the words flood over me.

"I hope Ruthy won't rush into marriage the way I did that first time. I felt so <u>desperate,</u> and I wanted someone to lean on. I pray she'll never feel that way. My parents thought that I needed to be married, but was that really true? What if I had never married? Would my life have been better?"

I felt a little sick; with these first words I had discovered something new. Mom's first marriage had been a true disaster — I had always known that — but I thought that she had loved my father. But this note, written ten years into their marriage, holds a definite note of regret. Was I prepared to find out why?

I dropped the letter and picked up another, written in a safely unfamiliar hand. The script was tight and slightly cramped. Dated 1925, it began "Dear Dadsy-boy," the brown ink wavering uncertainly on cream stationery. Mom's sister, I thought, the one who died long before I was born. "I'm glad I'm over here and not at home. It's so hard to keep pure ideals at home when all anybody talks about is society."

The letter went on, a virtuous little screed about living an upright life. This sister sounded like such a Goody Two-shoes, so different from my dynamic mother, that I began to wonder why Mom had loved her with such fierceness. Still trying to picture this long-dead aunt, I spotted the signature and realized that it did not belong to her after all: My mother, seventeen, had signed the letter. This was not the young Mom I had imagined, and I released the letter, heart beating, to peer down into the box.

It was utter chaos, a jumble of voices belonging to people who died long ago. Letters from dozens of different friends and family members, shopping lists, unused prescriptions and newspaper clippings were crammed in, helter-skelter. Time telescoped around me as I pulled out the yellowing bits of paper and began to read, rocketing dizzyingly from 1924 to 1988 and back again.

Mom did not keep what any normal person would call a diary, but constantly wrote notes on scraps of paper. They were threaded through the pile of letters like shouts from the past, eager to be heard. Who was she writing to? What was she trying to say? And would I have the courage to listen?

I wasn't sure. Looking for a sign, I closed my eyes and picked up a note at random, the way you open up a fortune cookie or consult a Magic

8-Ball. If the words told me to, I would close the box and let the past lie undisturbed. But if they beckoned me forward I would follow them and go searching for my mother.

I opened my eyes and looked at the note in my hand. Mom had been an old lady when she scrawled these words across the paper. "Who am I? What do I want? Why do I stand in my own way so often? It's not good enough to say that my mother thought self-analysis was self-indulgent. She's been dead for 25 years. I need to find me."

Could the message have been clearer? And so I began traveling through the box, trying to answer my mother's questions. As I sorted out the handwriting I got to know my grandparents, who both died when I was small. I discovered that my father was an ardent lover, a wonderful writer, and deeply romantic. But mostly I met my mother — as a little girl, a hopeful young woman and an increasingly unhappy older one. And the more I came to know this woman, the more grateful I became that I did not have to live her life.

Mom turned out to be very little like the comic character of the Mim Tales. She was more thoughtful, more self-aware and much more generous than I had ever appreciated. Getting to know her now, I realized how much I missed by not knowing her better when she was still alive.

But there was something more. As I came to know this new person, I began to see how much I owe her. Mom may not have realized her dreams, but that did not make her bitter. She did not have a happy life, but she wanted one for me. And she made enormous emotional sacrifices to make sure that my life would not turn out like hers.

WHAT GIRLS CAN DO

The earliest letter in the box comes at you like a slap. Even after eighty-four years its heartless candor leaves a bruise. Had my father written me a letter like that when I was sixteen I think I would have burned it on the spot. I know I would not have kept it. But Mom had carefully filed her father's letter away, and reading it now I tried to figure out why she had hung on to these brutal words for her entire lifetime.

"You are a dear girl," my grandfather had written, "and you have a fine mind. But you will have to resign yourself to the fact that you are homely. Finding a husband will not be easy."

It was a kind of curse that followed her always. In those few sentences he had hit on all the major issues that were to plague her life: She was smart but it did not really matter. She was handicapped because she was not pretty. And she would be a failure if she never married.

My grandparents, Emil and Mollie Brudno, were the children of immigrants who had come to Cleveland in the late 1800s, and they had exalted aspirations. By the time my mother was born in 1908 Emil had turned himself into a well-to-do doctor and Mollie was running his rather grand and extremely orderly house.

But what connected them and defined their lives was a shared and absolutely insatiable appetite for culture. They were wild for music, books and art (in that order), and they traveled widely. Throughout their lives they shared their thoughts, writing letters almost daily even when they were not apart.

When Mom was sixteen my grandmother took her two daughters to spend the year in Switzerland. I had always known that my mother was educated abroad, and I had always imagined that it was because my grandparents were pretentious snobs who wanted to emulate the "grand tour" of the aristocrats. I was wrong. Reading the letters I discovered that my grandmother was a prodigy who had been offered a scholarship to study music in Switzerland at the age of sixteen. Had she been a boy her parents would have let her go, but she was only a girl, so they made her turn it down and go to work so that she could put her only brother through college and then medical school. Now, with a devastated post-war Europe affordable for Americans, Mollie hoped to offer her daughters the experience that she herself had been denied.

Mom was not musical but she was a dutiful daughter, and she tried to be grateful. She wrote daily letters home to "Dadsy-boy," her unformed handwriting offering an eloquent picture of her days. She read good books. She took long walks. She played golf. And she practiced the violin for six hours full every day.

It is hard for me to imagine Mom screeching away at the violin; I never heard her play. Didn't she resent those long hours of practice? In a rare show of spirit she wrote, "I wish that man Kreutzer had never lived to write such horribly difficult exercises! I hate him." But not until Mom was in her fifties did she permit herself to give vent to her true feelings. "I was not musically gifted like my mother," she wrote then. "All I ever wanted was to be a doctor like my father. I was no good at the violin and I knew it. Why couldn't they let me *be?* I will never do this to my daughter."

But at seventeen she was still eager to please her parents, and so when her mother sailed home with her sister, Mom stayed on in Paris to pursue a doctorate in music. It sounds like such a lonely life: She had no friends and spent all her time practicing her violin and spending long hours at the Bibliothèque Nationale doing arcane musical research.

In her letters home she does not complain but endlessly thanks her parents for "the wonderful opportunity you are giving me." Mom's relentlessly saccharine letters are maddening: Being a teenager alone in a foreign country studying a subject you don't much like cannot have been fun, but she is humble, grateful, virtuous. "I have decided to read at least one classic book a week," she wrote to her father, "so that I can improve my mind." Meanwhile her sister, only a year and a half younger, is writing breathless letters about all the wonderful parties she's been invited to, and the great fun she is having at home.

"Why did I let my parents push me so?" Mom lamented in later life. "Why did I let them rob me of the chance to go to college in order to study something that I had no background in? Why didn't I listen to myself instead of them?" From this distance it is easy to see what was going on, but Mom was well into middle age before she came to the conscious realization that what she had been pursuing was her mother's dream.

"We are so proud of you!" her parents wrote when she passed her oral exams. And they were exultant when she breezed through the written ones and received her doctorate.

She was nineteen.

What she was expected to do with this is anybody's guess. The America my mother returned to in 1927 was still a polite turn-of-the-century society entirely dominated by men. I scrambled through the letters looking for some mention of the Nineteenth Amendment, some intimation that it had changed their lives, but there was nothing. Women might have earned the right to vote in 1920, but the amendment passed by a single vote and it actually changed very little. Lindbergh and his flight were dominating the news when Mom returned to America, and newspapers were running headlines like "Woman Suffrage Declared a Failure." And so once again my mother proved what a good girl she was. She returned home to live with her parents and search for a husband.

On the surface she was serene, but there was one significant sign of the rebellion to come: She put down her violin and never played another note. And then she finally did something that *she* wanted to do: She opened a bookshop. Why? "I was so lonely, and I longed for a life full of people," she wrote to a friend. "And I have always loved to read."

It was a bold move for the time. The day the shop opened her mother's good friend, the Reverend John Haynes Holmes, sent a note of encouragement and congratulations: "I admire the intelligence and courage that you are manifesting in the venture. You are showing what girls can do in this, our age."

Sitting at her desk Mom carried on a lengthy correspondence with some of the most interesting minds of her day. When I was a little girl I would sometimes surprise her in the living room, silently crying as she read those letters, over and over. She would not tell me why, but now I know that she was remembering her first step into independence, and a time when authors such as Christopher Morley had discussed their books with her and critics like Max Eastman told her their troubles. She corresponded with all kinds of people. There are dozens of letters from the leftist labor lawyer Aaron Sapiro about a scheme to change the way California farmers sold their fruit. Authors thanked her for her critiques of their books. And publishers flirted charmingly as they suggested titles for her shop. ("*The Red Badge of Courage,* just published this week, is a wow and is selling very well. I suggest that you push that and the *Time Machine,* which will be coming out in a fortnight. And by the way, are you married, single or contemplating?")

She was not contemplating, and it worried her. Time was passing. "I don't want to be one of those spinsters, those unmarried Aunts who are always an object of pity," she wrote. And then she added wistfully, "How I wish I were as pretty as my sister! I wonder how I will ever find someone to love me?"

And then in 1929 the tone of her letters got abruptly dark. The Depression, of course, changed life for everybody in America but Mom had gone into business on a lark, and she was fretting about receipts and sales and desperately trying to keep her little bookshop going. And then there was a worse disaster. Her sister fell precipitously ill with a diseased spleen and was dead within the week.

FINDING
MR. RIGHT

"I was smart and she was pretty," my mother always said when she spoke about her sister. "I never had the slightest doubt that as far as my parents were concerned, pretty was better. From the moment she was born people stopped them on the street to admire their beautiful baby. They were convinced that Ruth was going to make a brilliant marriage, and they never worried about her. Her death was such a blow!"

When Rabbi Stephen Wise heard the news he tried to console my grandparents. "It is too terrible to be true, that lovely radiant child fallen upon sleep!" he wrote. "I have always felt that to give up a loved child to death must be like being buried alive."

He obviously knew the family well. "After Ruth died we went into permanent mourning," my mother told me. "My parents felt that it would be a crime to enjoy ourselves without her. We never celebrated another birthday, holiday or anniversary. It was a particularly bitter blow for my folks, because she wasn't there, and what could they expect from me? I was useless; I couldn't even find a husband."

But now they had other worries; when the stock market crashed, the family lost everything and their financial situation grew increasingly precarious. My grandmother, with her husband's blessing, decided that it was her duty to help out. She became an impresario, the Cleveland representative of the Hurok organization, renting theaters and bringing great musicians from around the world to perform in them.

"She was beautiful, well organized and charming," Mom always said of her mother, and I could not miss the mingled notes of envy and admiration in her voice. "She could do anything, easily. She was very good at business, and she was soon surrounded by musicians — Yehudi Menuhin, Fritz Kreisler, Arthur Rubinstein. It was her dream come true."

Mollie not only presented the artists but also entertained them in her home. Dozens of letters mention her spectacular hospitality. It must have been quite a salon, for even Clarence Darrow wrote, "What a delightful time I had at your house. I was just telling Arthur Garfield Hayes that I don't know when a whole family has made such a hit with me before."

To Mom, who was living at home, her mother's new business offered distinct advantages. Tall, slim and darkly intense, she may have felt that she paled beside her dazzling mother, but others saw her differently. After an evening at the house one man wrote, "Go ahead into life, full-blooded, courageous and leap for the adventure. But you must do it soon — before the summer of your youth has cooled off into caution. You are magnificently charming — and you come like a torrent. But you will be spent on the futility of little things. You are not a watercolor. You are carved out of life — and there can be no petty hesitancies about you."

When Mollie brought Bertrand Russell to lecture in Cleveland he felt much the same and was so taken with Mom that he quickly made plans to return. Embarking on this subsequent tour he wrote in his small, precise handwriting, "I wonder whether you realize that the strongest hope I had in coming to America this time was the hope of getting to know you better? I have loved you from the first moment I saw you, and more each time."

Mom never got over the fact that Bertie Russell had been in love with her, and I immediately recognized the handwriting on those square blue envelopes. I can't remember a time when Mom was not reading and rereading his letters, trying to reassure herself that she was the same person who had fascinated the great philosopher. But at twenty-two she was merely flattered: Russell was nearing sixty, and although they became lifelong friends and correspondents, he was hardly marriage material. And her parents were turning up the pressure.

"How we pray for you to meet Him!" my grandmother wrote in 1928.

"Happy New Year," she wrote again in 1931, "and may you find the Mr. Right. It is our one prayer and hope and we think of it every moment."

"There was a new moon last night," she wrote in 1933, "and I prayed and prayed for Him. I dream that you will find a mate."

A few weeks later my grandfather weighed in. "Every woman needs to be married, and my dearest wish is that you will find the deep happiness that comes from having a partner to love and guide you."

The condescending tone of that letter made me want to grind my teeth, and I went hunting for some evidence that my mother might — even once — have considered another option. Did it ever cross her mind that she might not marry?

Nothing, in all her notes or letters, gives any indication that she considered the possibility of staying single. She had been back from France for eight years, thirty loomed on the horizon and she was afraid that no man would ever marry her. And then, finally, a beau appeared. In 1935, there is a sudden flurry of letters from a man in Pittsburgh.

His first, written in an even, careful hand, begins, "I realize how terrible I am at writing love letters. I don't know whether you should feel complimented or insulted at my evident lack of experience." Mom was in no position to be picky; she chose to be complimented and before long there was talk of engagement rings. "Please remember, Ernest," she wrote fiercely, "I <u>don't want</u> one."

Reading Ernest's bland letters it is easy to see what disaster lies ahead. They had absolutely nothing in common and I found myself shouting,

"Don't do it!"

But of course she did. After a whirlwind courtship she closed her shop and moved to Pittsburgh. "People are still breathless over your sudden departure and fatal decision," my grandmother wrote, in between descriptions of the latest concert.

Her parents must have known how wildly inappropriate this marriage was, but Mollie was all approval. "Music to our ears and the greatest wish fulfilled," she wrote when she learned that my mother was, as she put it, "well and truly married." She was even happier ten months later when the baby was born, enthusing, "Now you are a <u>real</u> woman!"

Mom wanted to name the baby for her sister, but Ernest persuaded her to forgo Rufus and settle for the more conventional Robert. He was a good baby, and she tried to be happy, but she was beginning to wonder if she had made a mistake. "I have everything I am supposed to want," she wrote on one of her scraps of paper. "A presentable husband. A beautiful baby boy. A fine house. Why do I feel so sloppy, disgruntled and unattractive? I feel just like Orphan Annie."

The months wear on and you can feel Mom's spirits dwindle as she shrivels into the marriage. "I can't talk to him!" she wrote. Instead she began writing letters to Ernest, pouring her dreams onto the paper. She wanted "a home filled with peace, a few understanding friends, books, music . . . and above all deep understanding between ourselves. I need that to make life worthwhile." She sounds so earnest, so wistful and so young.

But in his replies Ernest simply sounds baffled. All he wants is a compliant wife, and he releases a chorus of complaint. "I know your intentions are good but as I've told you before, you do not weigh your words carefully enough before speaking. I wonder if you will ever acquire this habit?" She is too reckless, too impetuous, too impatient. She does not keep a neat house. She must be more careful when she drives.

Reading their correspondence is like watching a train wreck in slow motion. She tries to conform to his pleasant respectability, but she always gets it wrong. Trying to serve food that will please him, she continually fails; his letters reproach her with forgotten gravy and invisible desserts. Before long he is stopping at his club to play tennis after work and staying on for supper.

In the end, Mom stopped apologizing. "I can feel myself growing more and more rebellious," she confessed to a friend. "Who cares about menus and the way they are cooked when there are so many more interesting things to think about?"

She described the marriage as "tempestuously unhappy," but women of that time did not walk out merely because they were miserable. And they certainly did not leave when there were children. I had always wondered how Mom managed to extricate herself from this sad situation, and now I discovered the secret: He left her.

"I don't think he ever loved me," Mom lamented to her parents after Ernest declared that marriage was not for him. But to herself she admitted an even harder truth, one that reveals how thoroughly her confidence had been shattered. "I think he married me because he was in love with my mother," she confessed. "She was so beautiful and so accomplished. What a disappointment I must have been!"

Her parents were shocked; divorce in those days was very rare. "Did you really try?" asked my grandmother accusingly when she found that Mom had taken the baby and moved to New York. "It was over so quickly!" The marriage had lasted less than two years.

But although Mom's pride was

wounded, she was relieved and she wasted no time on regret. "What a pleasure it is to be independent!" she scrawled across a piece of paper, the words so exuberant you can almost hear the "Hallelujah Chorus" blaring in the background. In short order she found a small apartment in Greenwich Village, a baby nurse and a job, and set out to create that life she had dreamed of, the one filled with books, music and understanding friends.

Talking about the time between her marriages, Mom always glowed. "I finally found myself in New York," she said, "and I actually began to like myself a little. And for the first time in my life men liked me too. Then, one night . . ." Mom's voice always got dreamily seductive when she reached this point in her story. "I came home from a party and looked into the mirror. And then I looked again. I realized that a miracle had occurred: I was pretty!"

Mom repeated this story to me again and again when I turned into a pudgy, awkward teenager. "You'll see," she said, "once you find out who you are you will find your beauty. You have to grow into your face. But I promise you this: you will."

Anyone who has been an ugly adolescent — and we are legion — knows that the hopeless feeling of being unlovely and unlovable never really goes away. No matter how much we are able to transform ourselves in later life it is always there, lurking right beneath the surface. No mother can banish that particular pain from her child's life. But my mother, who had been told as a teenager that she was too homely to be successful, was determined to try.

"How could I feel good about myself when the self-image my mother gave me was that I was sloppy, inefficient, homely, ungraceful and ungracious?" she wrote on one of her scraps of paper. "I carried that person around for so many years. I want to protect Ruthy from that."

At the time I was too mortified by my appearance to be aware of the gift that my mother was offering. With my squishy blob of a body and untamable hair I felt like the Pillsbury Doughboy topped with a pad of Brillo, and when I looked in the mirror I hated myself.

Mom understood. "It is so hard to

watch Ruthy going through this," she wrote, "because I know exactly what she's feeling. I wish I could send her to the hairdresser, have her nose fixed, or buy a dress that will make her graceful. But I know that none of that will work. All I can offer her is hope. It's one thing my parents didn't do for me."

Idle Aptitudes

Mom enjoyed her newfound freedom, but she spent the rest of her life regretting how little she had done with it. Even at seventy she was still lamenting that she had not used that time more productively. "When Ernest left me and I thought about building a career, why didn't I do it? I wanted to study psychiatry. Imagine how that would have changed my life! Why was I in such a hurry?"

Reading that, I muttered, "Why are you always so hard on yourself?" She was a single mother with very little money; how could she have possibly managed medical school? As it was, Mom was barely able to make ends meet.

Although it was the late thirties and the country was still mired in the Depression, Mom had found herself a small job in publishing. She told her parents that the work was "fascinating," but to her friends she admitted the truth. "I am a secretary, and a very inexperienced one at that," she wrote. "And my boss wants a very experienced one. I don't know how long he will keep me. The publishing business is very precarious. And I am only making $25 a week."

The rent on her apartment was $77 a month, and although Ernest sent her $50 a month in child support, she had to scrimp. Once the early thrill of independence wore off, Mom began to chafe at spending time in a dull, low-paying job. She wanted a real career. In 1940, she took action; buried in the bottom of the box I found an official-looking document from the Human Engineering Laboratory of the Stevens Institute of Technology in Hoboken.

The report is filled with technical jargon that a long-lost booklet ("An Objective Approach to Group-Influencing Fields") apparently explains. Her test results indicate that she was terrible at both inductive and analytical reasoning and that she lacked all aptitude for accounting. But her creative imagination was high and her tonal memory almost perfect. "You have made 47 correct answers out of a possible 48," concluded the tester, Evelyn C. Wight, as she suggested that Mom consider work that combined her talents for words and music. "You must use your most outstanding characteristic in choosing a career," she cautioned. "Idle aptitudes cause restlessness and may detract from a woman's success and happiness."

In conclusion Ms. Wight suggested that Mom seek work with an agency doing public relations for musicians. The irony was not lost on Mom, but it was too late for her go into business with her mother.

When the Depression ended, so did my grandmother's fabulous career. She told her family that she folded her business because no woman worked unless she had to. "She didn't want people to think that Dr. Emil couldn't support her," Mom told me. I think that my mother believed that, but it was not the truth.

There were a few cryptic letters from famous people in the box, and as I struggled to find out what they meant I discovered that Mollie did not walk away from her job — it was wrenched out from under her. Culture is not an easy sell in hard times, and at the start of the Depression Cleveland's impresario went looking for a more lucrative career. (His daughter thinks he survived by selling nasal preparations.) When prosperity returned, he wanted his job back. And despite my grandmother's success, he got it. "Did my father play on sensibilities at the time that he had a young wife and three little children to support and Mollie didn't?" his daughter wonders. "I don't know."

My grandmother fought back, trying to create a business without the blessing or backing of the big New York organization. "What a pity that the cancellation in your course is such a problem," wrote Ezio Pinza. "I would love to help you out of your difficulty . . ." Other artists offered help as well; Rudolf Serkin even offered money. But it was an uphill battle, and after a few more attempts Mollie gave up. Her career was over, and although whining was not her way, I don't think she ever recovered.

But things were finally looking up for Mom. Just after her excursion to the Human Engineering Laboratory she met my father at a party and fell instantly in love. Ernst Reichl was a quietly elegant intellectual who had fled his wealthy German-Jewish family because he had absolutely no desire to go into any of the businesses they owned. Lacking any talent for money, he persuaded his family to let him get a PhD in literature. And then he came to America to pursue his passion for books. When he met Mom he was convinced that she was a kindred spirit, and immediately began planning a life with her.

"Terribly busy and happy," Mom wrote giddily to her parents in the first month of their marriage. "I'll write tomorrow."

Dad was endlessly admiring. He thought Mom was the smartest, kindest, most generous and most passionate woman he had ever met, and he never stopped telling her so. His letters are filled with the incredible joy of having found her; he could not believe his luck and she blossomed beneath his appreciation.

"I wish," he wrote, "that I had your jubilant self confidence, your supreme assurance that what is good for you and yours is the right, the good, the only thing to do. I am going to lean heavily on your strength."

The war years were a good time for strong women. Dad was too old to be called up, so he moved into her small apartment, squeezing in with my brother, then eight, and his little dog, Tippy. My parents pooled their resources, found an investor and created a small publishing company to produce handwritten literary books.

In the first photograph taken in their new office Mom looks so happy.

Her dark hair is pulled straight back, and she wears perilously high heels, seamed nylons, a slim skirt and no makeup as her fingers fly across a typewriter. They had very little money but they didn't care. They were together, doing work that they both believed in, and for the first few years the letters are ecstatically happy.

But the calligraphy series did not do very well, so they changed directions and produced a twelve-volume series called *The Homemaker's Encyclopedia,* which was written entirely by my mother. It included volumes on needlecraft, home repairs, gardening, housekeeping, entertaining — even personal beauty and charm. How my mother, who could not cook, had never sewn a single garment, gardened not at all, despised cleaning and used no makeup, managed to produce this vintage gem still baffles me. "It was a challenge," she said proudly. "But I have always been good at research. And" — she could never resist adding this — "it made a fair amount of money."

They finished the series just after I was born, and then they started a magazine for brides. But that did not do very well either, and by then their financial needs had become pressing. My father's parents, who had escaped Hitler by fleeing to Shanghai, had finally made their way to America and were exhausted, ill and destitute. Desperately trying to support them, my parents sold their company. They thought that Dad could earn more doing the work that he was known for — designing books. And I can't help thinking that after his stint with homemakers and brides Dad must have been secretly happy to return to the literature that he loved.

Mom ran his office for a while but she knew nothing about typography and could do little more than answer phones and type invoices. Before long she realized that she was back where she had been when they met: doing dull, routine chores that neither exploited her talents nor engaged her mind.

Dad encouraged her to find other work, but after the war jobs for women were not easy to come by. In fact, women who worked were considered unpatriotic. "You women and girls go home, back to being housewives as you promised to do," trumpeted an army general in a widely televised speech. In the background you can hear the men cheering wildly. Little wonder, then, that by the time I was old enough to notice, Mom was not working at all.

And, with the exception of a couple of widows and the women she pityingly called "career spinsters," none of her friends were either. All of those smart, competent women sat at home, twiddling their thumbs and telling their daughters how much they had enjoyed working during the war.

CHAOS

Whenever my mother's parents came to visit our cramped apartment my mother flew into a panic. She would go rushing through the rooms like Hurricane Miriam, flinging things from every drawer and closet. Playing with my toys I would find myself surrounded by heaps of clothes, piles of linens, stacks of books and towers of plates, while my mother, her now-graying hair tied up in a scarf, madly ran the vacuum cleaner through the clutter as if that could somehow make it magically disappear.

"They'll be here in three hours!" she'd cry, terror in her voice. Even at four I understood that "they" were the old people who appeared on our doorstep from time to time. Mom always undertook a cleaning binge right before her parents arrived, a kind of mad last-minute frenzy that never left enough time to repair the mess that she had made.

When the bell rang, Mom's eyes always went wide. And there they'd be, my grandfather with his elegant shock of white hair and my impeccably regal grandmother. They would stroll in, look at each other in dismay and sadly shake their heads. From the floor I'd look up, hating them but not really knowing why.

I resented my grandmother and dreaded her visits. I used to think it was because they made our crowded apartment feel even smaller than it really was. But now I know that whenever she showed up our apartment turned into a battleground where two deeply disappointed women waged a war that was especially fierce because it had been such a long time coming.

The combatants themselves were conscious of the struggle, and they knew exactly where the lines were drawn. After one especially acrimonious visit Mom wrote this letter to my grandmother.

"Mother Darling: You and I always laughed when everyone told me that I acted like a little girl towards my parents. That, at my present middle-age, I can no longer do.

"You continually reproach me when

I don't live up to your expectations. Please try to treat me as a passably intelligent adult who should be mature enough to manage her own, and her children's lives."

She was forty-five years old, and she had spent her entire life trying to win her parents' approval. She had gotten a doctorate just to please them, she had married a suitable man and she had borne her due allotment of children. And yet none of that had been enough. Her mother demanded unconditional admiration, holding herself up as the ideal model and expecting Mom to follow in her footsteps. Mom had certainly tried. The problem was, she was not equipped to do it.

My grandmother did not — or could not — see this. "Thank you for your explanation of your attitude to me," she wrote back. "I always try to understand, and some of it may be my fault. I am very hard on you because I loathe disorder and just can't take a harsh voice. I have given you the very best that I know how . . . and you aren't grateful enough for what you have."

Disorder and harsh voices were beside the point, and Mom knew it. But gratitude was something else. "I <u>am</u> ungrateful," she wrote in one of her more desperate notes. "I know it. Everything is easier now. Our financial obligations have lessened and Ernst is finally making enough for us to live on. My children are healthy. But everything is such a mess. I hate keeping house! My meals are awful. I wasn't cut out for this. I wish I knew what to do!"

Her unhappiness was palpable and it drove everyone from the house. My grandparents' visits became less frequent. My anguished father tried to soothe her; I think he would have done anything to make Mom happy but their financial needs forced him to work longer and longer hours, and he often skipped dinner to eat a sandwich at his desk. My big brother begged his father to send him to boarding school. Long before Bob went off to college he was spending most of his time in Pittsburgh, and his visits home became rare treats.

Trying to keep herself occupied, Mom threw herself into entertaining. She rearranged our apartment, replacing all the beds with pull-out sofas so that each room was party-ready. "It's so convenient," she explained when I protested that I would prefer sleeping on a bed. "We can have cocktails in the living room, dinner in our bedroom and dessert in yours!"

Mom's novel entertaining scheme involved more than a moveable feast: While her guests drifted from room to room, she served what she called "interesting dishes they would not forget." To that end she tried turning herself into a cook, pouncing upon every unfamiliar food that crossed her path. She discovered sea urchins at the fish market, their bristles still sharp and dangerous, and brought them home along with a smooth cactus flower she had unearthed in Little Italy. She found slick, perfumed lychee nuts in Chinatown, and one morning I opened the refrigerator to find an entire baby piglet staring out at me.

The fact that Mom had no idea how to deal with these novelties did not worry her. She was, after all, the editor of *The Homemaker's Encyclopedia,* and her creativity was endless: Once she managed to combine canned asparagus with mayonnaise, Marshmallow Fluff and some leftover herring to make an hors d'oeuvre. It was painful to watch people eating these dishes, and I soon appointed myself the guardian of the guests, intent on making sure that nobody got sick on Mom's more outlandish experiments. When my exhausted father begged Mom to cease entertaining I was delighted.

For a few embarrassing months she

became the leader of my Brownie troop. It began well: At first she organized us into a roving band of players who went around the city acting out the Bemelmans story *Madeline* in hospitals. But after the initial excitement wore off she lost interest, and when one of the other mothers reported what she had offered us as snacks, Brownie Headquarters asked Mom to step down.

She took on volunteer jobs — Mom would eventually end up doing stints at the Red Cross, the Girl Scouts, UNICEF, the Silvermine Guild of Artists, the Metropolitan Museum and the New York Public Library. But these jobs never lasted. She was not looking for something that would fill her time or make a little money; she was still in search of a meaningful career.

Like everyone else in the family, I did my best to avoid Mom. I would come home from school in the afternoon, put my key in the lock and pray that she was out. I dreaded the dead air in the apartment, which was heavy with unhappiness. I dreaded the endless questions about what I had done that day. The rest of the family had fled, and Mom sat at home like a caged tiger with a dangerously twitching tail. When I walked in, she pounced, demanding little pieces of my life.

It was on one of those leaden afternoons that Mom first told me that she had wanted to be a doctor. And it was then that she said, for the first of many times, "My parents said that if I went to medical school I would never find a husband. What a fool I was to listen to them!"

At the time I could feel the deep bitterness behind her words, and I understood how much she resented the limits her parents had put upon her life. But now I see that she was not talking about herself. She was sending me a message, telling me not to make the same mistakes that she had. In an act of extraordinary generosity she was offering me another gift that she had been denied: She was giving me permission to defy her.

And although I did not know it then, I heard her loud and clear.

WHAT WE ARE
MADE FOR

Mom drove her family crazy, but she was relentlessly social and a very good friend to a surprisingly broad spectrum of people. Among her many women friends my favorite, at least when I was small, was her childhood friend Hermine.

She was everything my mother wasn't. An immensely successful businesswoman, she lived in a fabulous apartment just off Fifth Avenue. Tall, thin and elegant, she dressed gorgeously in handmade clothes that always looked as if they were being worn for the first time. Her shoes always gleamed with polish and her stockings never ran.

As a little girl I considered her sunken living room the utmost in sophistication and I'd jump up the stairs, just for the pleasure of going back down, imagining myself sweeping into a room the way Auntie Mame did in the movies. Sometimes I even recited her line "Life's a banquet and most poor suckers are starving to death" as I walked in.

Unlike the messy apartment in which my family lived, Hermine's place was always serenely immaculate. Her housekeeper, Mildred, ironed the sheets, put clean towels in the bathrooms and made sure that the tables were polished to a luxurious sheen. Every time I walked through the door I inhaled deeply; I loved the way Hermine's apartment smelled, an irresistible mixture of flowers, furniture wax, sugar and butter. I'd follow the aroma through the living room, admiring the beautiful bouquets nodding in their vases, into the old-fashioned kitchen, where Hermine could often be found baking her famous cookies. She was a legendary cook, and I was always hanging around, dropping desperate hints to be invited to stay for supper.

But as a very little girl I understood that despite all this Hermine was a person to be pitied. As the door closed behind us my mother always sighed and said, "What a waste! Poor Hermine is a spinster." And each time Mom met an unmarried man she'd look him speculatively up and down and ask my father, "Do you think he might like Hermine?"

I was almost twelve before a man who *did* like Hermine came along. Mom had introduced them, and she was very proud when they got married.

Joe moved into Hermine's apartment, and before long the lovely aroma of flowers and sugar was overwhelmed by a heavy fog of tobacco that hung in the air. Joe didn't want his wife working outside the home, so Hermine quit her job. And one day when Mom and I stopped in we found that Mildred was gone. "Oh, darling," said Hermine when I asked, "Joe didn't like having a strange woman in the house. And he didn't see any reason to pay someone to clean when I am perfectly capable of doing it myself."

Walking home, I knew that Mom was having second thoughts about the miracle she'd wrought. "Her shoes weren't even shined!" she cried. "In my whole life I've never seen Hermine looking so unkempt." She sighed unhappily. "Do you think she would have been better off if she hadn't gotten married?"

Mom said nothing more on the subject, at least to me. But when I found this note I realized she had written it upon returning from our final afternoon at Hermine's. "I am so sorry I did not pursue a career. If I teach Ruthy nothing else, I must make her see this. In the end, it is meaningful work — serving people — that matters most. It is what we were made for."

Mom made new friends, and I was especially fond of Flora. Her husband had been a manufacturer of girls' dresses until he dropped dead at the age of thirty-two, leaving her with two small children. "She had never even been inside the factory," my mother told me, "but at the funeral one of the men came up to ask if she planned on closing down." Seeing how frightened he was about losing his job, Flora tried to reassure him. She told him that the factory would carry on. He asked who was going to run the business. "To her surprise," Mom said, "Flora said that she would."

"And then what?" I always asked. I loved this story.

"The next day she went into the factory and told the men that she would need their help, but that together they were going to keep the factory going. And it turned out that she was a wonderful manager and an even better businesswoman; today the business is four times the size it was when Lou was alive. The funny thing is that if Lou hadn't passed away she would have been just another bored housewife."

I remember exactly where I was when my mother said that, and I can hear her tone of voice. But what I remember most is what she didn't say: "A bored housewife like me."

My other favorite among Mom's friends was also a widow. But Claudia had no children, and she had not gone to work because she needed money. She had gone to work strictly for the fun of it.

The first time Mom told the tragic story she whispered it into my ear as if it were too terrible to say out loud. Long ago Claudia had fallen in love with a wonderful man, and they had been married in a wedding at the Plaza. It had all the trimmings — an organ, an aisle, a father's arm, clouds of white lace and a cake of many tiers. They had honeymooned in Spain.

"But Bert was a producer," said Mom, "and one night as he was coming home from the theater a taxi veered out of control, jumped onto the sidewalk and hit him as he stood waiting for the light. He was killed instantly. Claudia thought her life was over. She was so devastated that she took to her bed and stayed there for months. It was awful. None of us knew what to do. We tried to lure her out of her apartment, but she wouldn't budge."

"So what did you do?" I asked.

"Not a thing," Mom said. "One day I called and she wasn't there. She had gone back to work. She had been an acting coach before she married, and she decided that the only way to get over her sadness was to pick up where she left off."

And so Claudia worked with the stars. She was very busy, traveling endlessly around the world. Each time Mom returned from lunch wearing the scarf, or the pin, or the gloves that Claudia had brought back from her latest sojourn to Rome or Paris, she always seemed slightly wistful. "Claudia has a career. She does exactly what she wants and answers to no one but herself," she told me on one of those afternoons.

That was all she said. It was enough.

DEAR
DR. PORTNOY

As Mom grew older her despair deepened and she became increasingly erratic. Sometimes she was so filled with manic energy that she didn't sleep at all. Waking in the middle of the night, I'd hear her fingers tapping on the typewriter, or the vacuum cleaner sucking up dust in the dark. But other times she'd refuse to get out of bed, lying prone for weeks on end, unwilling to leave her room. Dad was puzzled, and he watched her with anxious eyes, wishing he had some way to make her happy.

I could sense his relief when she was in a good mood, and he always chose to be amused by her giddier schemes. He laughed when she painted the bathroom gold, even though every bath left us slightly gilded. He thanked her for each outrageous meal, loyally insisting that she was a wonderful cook. And when she bought a painting we could not afford, he said, as he took on extra work, that it was sure to be a good investment. But when she stayed in bed for months he gently suggested that she see a psychiatrist.

"Doctor Portnoy says . . ." became a common refrain around our house, and I came to hate the sound of his name. The man seemed to have opinions on a startlingly wide range of subjects, and Mom used him to justify every action.

"Doctor Portnoy thinks this party is a very good idea," she announced as she informed us of her plans to celebrate my brother's engagement. Bob, who was twenty-six and working on Wall Street, was horrified to learn that Mom intended using the occasion to raise funds for her latest cause, UNICEF. She had invited two hundred paying guests to meet his new family at our shabby house in the country. "I'm going to cater the whole thing myself," she cried enthusiastically. "That way I can raise more money for the needy children!"

"No experiments," Bob groaned, "please!"

"Don't worry," Mom promised, "you'll be able to recognize every single thing I serve." She neglected to mention that in the interests of efficiency she was going to prepare the food ahead of time; we lacked adequate refrigeration and it was the height of summer.

The whole affair was a horrible nightmare. Bob and I spent the party running from table to table, doing our best to keep people from eating the scariest dishes. But despite our efforts the party ended with a couple of dozen people in the hospital; they were having their stomachs pumped.

"Nonsense," said Mom when Bob called to inform her that his future in-laws were ill. "We all feel fine." Then she locked herself in the bathroom and plunked herself into the tub. Over the sound of the running water she shouted, "Doctor Portnoy will be so pleased by all the money

I've raised."

I thought the episode had moved seamlessly from disaster to family legend, one of those stories repeated yearly at Thanksgiving. I did not know that Mom had ever given her party another thought. But a few days afterward she wrote this letter:

Dear Dr. Portnoy:
It seems to me that sometimes a psychiatrist, like another kind of doctor or a dentist, might say, "This is going to hurt. It has to be done sometime or other, so we might as well do it now." I don't know whether such a warning would break the shock, I do know that I haven't come to since last Tuesday. The time was ripe, I agree, even over-ripe. But there ought to be some

kind of anesthetic for times when you cut so pitilessly deep into pride, ridicule, etc. I don't have to spell it out for you. For it wasn't done impulsively or hostilely. It was a planned, necessary part of the treatment.

To make matters even more difficult after such an eye-opening, revealing portrayal as you painted, you can't allow silence. That would be considered hostile on my part. After silences you've chided me with, "I'll keep silent and see how he likes that," or "Of course you can talk, you're talking when you say I can't talk."

Sometimes it's a privilege to keep silent, to be allowed to crawl into one's shell and lick one's wounds in private. But thank you for your effort — which I know it was. It was a most rewarding session.

And I've dredged several things out of me since. One — that dignity is jeopardized by these episodes which make one feel ridiculous, and which I haven't been able to put a stop to.

Two — Sometimes it will be worth my while to appear ridiculous. But it won't be those impulsive actions, it will be a considered risk.

And three — sometimes fifty people are better than four people and 200 people better than 50. If one is trying to raise money for a movement.

Is that defiance?

She signed the letter "Miriam" in a savage, slashing hand. As far as I can tell it was never mailed. Or maybe Mom typed up another copy and kept the original as a warning to herself, an attempt to prevent future episodes. The letter made me ache for her, and I reread it over and over, wondering what she meant about the considered risk. Who would ever want to be consciously ridiculous? How could that ever be worth anyone's while? What was she talking about?

If Dr. Portnoy asked those questions, she did not note it. But he was clearly not a doctor who sat silent as his patients rattled on. In another one of her notes Mom wrote: "Psychiatrists seemed to feel anyone could be cured by psychoanalysis if one stuck with it and was cooperative. So one went year after year. One year, two, three, four, five and six. He berated, ridiculed, teased and scolded using every torturous weapon at his command. 'Other people get well; why can't you? Why do you have to repeat the same monotonous pattern over and over? I'm so bored with it.' He assured you that he knew what you were going to say at each session before you said it. How tiresome you were!"

Would he have been equally condescending if Mom had been a man? And how many more years would this treatment have continued if Mom had not read an article about a new field of medicine? Psychopharmacology was still in the experimental stages, but she was intrigued by a cure that required no talking, and eagerly offered herself up to science.

"How comforting it is to hear that I am not to blame for my difficulties!" she wrote after the first visit. "Dr. Malitz believes that they are beyond my control. And he assures me that he will give me medication that will help."

What he gave her was lithium, a drug not approved by the FDA until 1970. She also took dozens of other drugs — Elavil, Ritalin, Atavil, Thorazine, Librium, Doriden, Norpramin, Vivactil, Aventyl, Tofranil . . . Over the next fifteen years she visited half a dozen different doctors, each attempting to cure her with various combinations of drugs. One doctor, she wrote, was extremely kind and called her daily to check up on her progress. One reminded her of Dr. Portnoy. And another ran what she called a factory. "He has so many patients waiting for their five minutes with the doctor that the staff can't keep our medicines straight. I am always worried that they are going to give me the wrong pills."

None of this came as a surprise to me; my mother never minimized her mental problems. "This is no way to live," she told me over and over as she apologized and downed her pills. "I don't want you to think that this is normal. Remember this: Just because I am this way, it doesn't mean that you will be."

Mom was not the only one on pills; she was just one of the millions of drugged mid-century Americans. A fifties ad for Dexedrine pictured a sad, pretty young woman holding a dishtowel and surrounded by dirty dishes. "Why is this woman tired?" asked the copy. "Many of your patients — particularly housewives — are crushed under a load of dull, routine duties that leave them in a state of mental and emotional fatigue. For these patients, you may find Dexedrine an ideal prescription. Dexedrine will give them a feeling of energy and well-being, renewing their interest in life and living."

A sixties ad for Dexamyl depicted a woman wearing an ecstatic smile as she vacuumed her house. "Mood elevation is usually apparent within 30 to 60 minutes," it enthused.

These were far from temporary remedies. My mother-in-law was given Benzedrine to help her cope with the tragic death of her young husband when she was in her early twenties. Betty was still dutifully taking the pills when I met her; by then she was in her fifties and her first husband was just a fuzzy memory. She had been remarried for more than twenty years, and she had two grown children. She was a conservative, churchgoing Midwesterner who thought of her daily pills as little more than vitamins; she would have been shocked to learn that she was a drug addict.

Drugs did help some people, but they brought my mother no peace. Although she was eventually diagnosed as manic-depressive it is impossible to know if she was clinically ill or merely a victim of what the woman at the Human Engineering Lab had called "idle aptitudes." Was she crazy, or was she crazy because she had nothing to do?

I don't know. I do know that she worried that the same fate would befall me, and she protected me in the only way that she knew how: by being honest. "I am so sorry," Mom kept repeating. "I know it is hard on you that I do such ridiculous and foolish things."

That could not have been easy to admit. Now I think it is what she meant by "the worthwhile risk," the one that was not impulsive. As a little girl I had done my best to protect the world from my mother and my mother from herself. But as I grew older I began to resent cleaning up the messes that she made with her inept housekeeping, her poisonous food and her crazy parties. I wanted nothing so much as to be different from her. And that is exactly what she wanted too.

My grandmother had tried to turn her daughter into a carbon copy of herself. That had not worked out well. And so my mother did the opposite: Instead of holding herself up as a model to be emulated, she led by negative example, repeating "I am a failure" over and over, as if it were a mantra. "I am ridiculous. Don't be like me. Don't be like me."

I can hardly imagine how excruciating that must have been. Parents yearn for their children's respect; most of us want it more than anything else on earth. And yet my mother deliberately sabotaged my respect and emphasized her failings. She loved me enough to make me love her less. She wanted to make sure that I would not follow in her footsteps.

It was an enormous sacrifice. She made it willingly. And I never even thanked her.

RAINBOWS

I could not wait to escape from my mother's unhappiness. At sixteen I took off for a college halfway across the country, and from then on returned home as little as possible. When I graduated I was so terrified of getting caught once again in my mother's orbit that I applied to graduate school.

But in 1970 I finally went home. I was about to be married, and I thought the least I could do was introduce my future husband to my parents.

111

Dad was very pleased. He reached to pat Doug on the back — they were exactly the same size — and within minutes they had disappeared into the study and a conversation that would last for the rest of my father's life. Meanwhile Mom and I went into the kitchen to start dinner, and as the lobsters crawled across the counter I noticed that her hair was now entirely white and she was thickening around the middle. "Isn't this very old-fashioned?" she asked, coolly stuffing the creatures into a pot. "I thought that these days people your age just lived together."

I was certain that Mom would eventually warm to the idea. She did not. She wouldn't help me plan the wedding, and she refused to buy herself a dress. During the weeks leading up to the event she groused about every aspect of the affair, from the fact that we were planning to recite our vows on a stretch of unfinished highway ("Why do you want to do it in the road?") to my insistence on baking my own cake ("You know I have no pans"). When ten friends drove across the country and pitched their tents on the front lawn, she was not amused. "Why didn't you just elope?" she asked crossly.

I should not have been surprised. Mom had hated being pressured into marriage, and she had scrupulously avoided doing the same thing to me. She had introduced me to her friends, shown me the drawbacks of a traditional marriage and offered me what she herself had wanted — permission not to marry. Now I was throwing it all away. Aggressively: Of all my friends I was the first to tie the knot.

She must have considered this an enormous rejection, and I suppose that was the point. She had trained me to be defiant, but this was an unanticipated consequence. Her response to my marriage was her way of jumping up and down, shouting, "This isn't what I meant!"

Still, she saved the wedding announcement. On the front is a picture of Doug and me, standing on the bare dirt of the highway on which we were married. Earthmovers loom over us. My dress is a rainbow, there are colorful ribbons in my hair and I am clutching a bunch of wild daisies. Inside is the service that we had written together.

"Your marriage must be a vow to encourage each other to realize his own best qualities. You believe that you have found a person who will stretch your own limits, one who will provide a constantly challenging dialogue to encourage you each to grow in his own direction. You do not come to this marriage to find a resting place."

Reading that, I thought how very sixties it sounded. But then I went back to the letter Mom had written, so hopefully, to her first husband thirty-five years earlier. She had wanted "an atmosphere of understanding," a partnership, something very different than the "guidance" her father had so earnestly hoped a husband would offer her. There was an echo there, and it must have been bittersweet to watch me embark on exactly the sort of marriage that she herself had never achieved.

Mom apparently intended to send the announcement to a friend, because on the back she had written, "Ruth is now Mrs. Douglas Hollis. The wedding was completely unconventional. I hope the marriage will be too. But we all start off with such high hopes and look where we end up."

Reading that brought back another memory. The night before the wedding, Mom came to my room to watch me try on my dress. She gulped when she saw the many layers of color, but managed to say "It's lovely," in a voice that sounded sincere. Then she cleared her throat and added, "I know you don't need any advice on birds and bees. But you do know that you're going to become a new person, don't you?"

"What do you mean?" I asked.

"Once you're married," she replied, "you will stop being Ruth Reichl and start being Mrs. Douglas Hollis."

Now I realize that she was being provocative, mischievously throwing out a lure. She knew how much I hated the idea of losing both my names, of disappearing into someone else's identity. Oblivious, I took the hook.

"I don't want to be a new person!" I shouted. "Don't you ever call me by that name! I'm still me. If you ever send a letter addressed to Mrs. Douglas Hollis I swear I will return it unopened."

It was a challenge that Mom was

incapable of resisting. And there, in the bottom of the box, was the envelope with "return to sender" scrawled across the front. It was still sealed.

Curious, I slit it open.

Mom had known I wouldn't read it: She had written the letter to herself.

It begins, "Why did I always do what my parents felt that I should do and not listen to my own feelings?" On the following page she listed all the mistakes that she had made in her life. But it ends on an optimistic note. "Your children are grown. From this day on you <u>must</u> stop looking back and move forward. It's a new world."

I wish that I had opened the letter; Mom had obviously been hoping that I would, because this was more than a reminder that a lot still lay ahead of her. Mom was writing to me, too, cheering me on and pointing out that I had an obligation, both to myself and to her, to use my life well. She understood that we had both come to a crossroads, and she was hoping that we would both head in the right direction.

Tsunami of Pain

Energized, Mom marched bravely into the future. She sent out dozens of letters that began, "I am the editor of the twelve volume set, The Homemaker's Encyclopedia," to one group of prospects. To another group she wrote letters that called on her musical background. But she was now in her sixties, and all that came back were polite rejections. She wrote a few book proposals as well, but they went nowhere.

For a while she became a full-time volunteer at the Metropolitan Museum of Art, but she took umbrage at being treated as inferior to the paid employees. She wanted to be a curator, and while she tried to fool her friends ("I have the most fascinating new job!") she could not fool herself. Frustrated, angry and increasingly frightened about her future, she picked fights with everyone.

She began with the people who ran the volunteer program at the museum, eventually becoming so contentious that she was asked to leave. Next she turned on me. Doug and I were living in New York, and when I got the contract to write my first book I went to my parents' apartment to share the good news. Mom's reaction was chilling. "Do you think we sent you to graduate school so you could write cookbooks?" she asked. "When are you going to do something worthwhile?"

Then it was Bob's turn; she did not approve of his lifestyle, his values or the way he was bringing up her grandchildren. "I've been heartbroken about the way you treat me," she began one letter. Another ended, "So I've stopped crying. What choice do I have?"

"My children have abandoned me," she wailed after Bob and I both fled New York, unwilling to stay and endure her increasingly angry despair. But even her friends were not immune. "I've realized," she wrote on one of those endless scraps of paper, "that I really don't like Bert: He's arrogant, undependable, contemptuous, dull and neurotic. And Jean is frivolous, calculating, a social climber, predatory, ambitious for the wrong things."

Reading through this tsunami of pain, I couldn't help wondering what it was about this particular point in Mom's life that had caused such an extreme reaction. She had been unhappy in the past, but never before had she turned on everyone. What was different now?

I think that the moment when the last child marries and leaves home is a milestone for every parent. It is a turning point and an inexorable reminder of mortality. But for the women of my mother's generation it must have been especially painful. Mom and her friends had poured so many of their hopes and aspirations into their daughters, and now they were watching us walk off into the future, leaving them behind.

In their letters Mom's friends all brag shamelessly about their children. The girls are becoming doctors and lawyers, and their mothers are both pleased and pained. "How wonderful that Nancy is a doctor," Mom wrote to one old friend. "She manages a house and two children as well; you must be so proud! Even when she was a child you could see what a capable woman she would become. I can't get over how different their world is from ours."

Mom sneered at my food career when she spoke to me, but her letters have a different tone. To one friend she wrote, "Ruthy has published a book. It's just a cookbook, but it is the first of what we hope will be many more books." She sent a review of the book to another friend, with a note that said, "We think she may have a real future as a writer!"

Reading that now, thirty-five years later, I can hear how the words come through gritted teeth and feel how unfair she considers all this. Indeed, an angry letter to my brother inadvertently revealed her true feelings. "You think that I'm a slob," she wrote. "You would probably think the same of Ruth if you saw her house in Berkeley. It is not neat but it is filled with art, culture and interesting friends. She is an independent person, working hard at writing, and she is supporting herself. She and I both think it is more important to do interesting work than to shop, cook, and clean."

But she, of course, was not doing

interesting work. She was shopping, cooking, cleaning. Her parents had passed away, her husband was busy and her children were gone. Peering into the future, she saw only emptiness. But she was not ready to give up. "My life is not over," she admonished herself. "I must work harder."

It was a wish as much as an exhortation, but circumstances intervened to make the wish come true. One of Dad's employees embezzled a large amount of money, putting his business into sudden jeopardy, and he asked Mom to find a temporary job. "Just until I get back on solid ground," he pleaded.

Mom was nothing if not resourceful, and she took herself off to the Department of Aging. "I can't imagine that they'll have anything for someone like me," she said dismissively. She was wrong. They offered her a job at the Library for the Performing Arts at Lincoln Center, and for the first time in her life my mother was doing work that employed both her training and her talents.

Dad's business recovered but Mom would not consider giving up her job. She was at her desk when she learned that my father had suffered a sudden stroke. A few days later he was gone. Mom threw herself into planning the memorial service, but when it was over she fell into a deep depression.

She stopped working, calling in sick until it was clear that she would never go back to the library. She did not return her calls, and eventually the phone stopped ringing. She no longer left the house, and all but stopped breathing. She was inconsolable. Bob and I had no idea what we ought to do, but as the years went on we both worried that she would never recover.

GRATEFUL

Dear Editor:

My name is Miriam Reichl. I am 77 years old and now live alone in New York City, in the same apartment I've lived in for 43 years. You must have many readers who have the same problems I have, who don't quite know how to cope now. Years ago we had husbands and children living at home, family meals to plan and serve, active social lives. And then, boom! — our husbands died and the bubble burst.

When my husband died my

daughter did what he'd always done for me: kept my financial affairs in order. But she had to do more than he did because now I just lay in bed, often with the covers over my head, wishing I could die. I let the mail, including bills and checks, lie around any old place, piling up.

For months I didn't even get dressed to fetch food and there were many times that my frig and cupboard were completely bare. My clothes were in shambles. I didn't buy anything new for four years.

I slept a lot, and procrastinated as much as possible. After all, I had no control over my life, did I? I even put off making beauty appointments until it was too late and the salon was all booked up. Then I felt so unkempt that I was too embarrassed to go anyplace, so I just stayed home.

And then — just as suddenly as I gave up — I came back to life. What happened? I realized that so many people had so many more problems than I did that it behooved me to be grateful.

I'd like to tell my story to your readers, so that they too can experience the same miraculous recovery.

The manuscript ends there. I imagine it is because Mom did not know what to say next. She couldn't tell anyone how to experience the miraculous recovery, because she had no idea how it had happened to her.

It was not drugs. She stopped taking them long before my father died.

She did occasionally see a psychiatrist, but he was a man who treated her with nothing but kindness. His sympathetic ear was surely helpful, but he was not the reason behind the great transformation. The real catalyst was something that Mom could not admit, even to herself.

This was the first time in her life that she had ever lived alone, and once Mom finished mourning my father, she thrived on it. You could see it just by looking at her. She wrote in a note, "People tell me that I've never looked better." It was true. Nearing eighty, with thick white hair and a vivacious smile, she had turned into a very beautiful old lady. She stopped caring what people thought and started wearing outlandish clothes of many colors. She draped herself with costume jewelry and delighted in her own eccentricity. Mom had always talked easily to strangers, and now she made new friends each time she boarded a bus. She met people everywhere she went — in the grocery store, at the movies, just walking through the park. But most of all she stopped berating herself for all the things she hadn't done — and she switched off the voice inside her head.

"My mother is dead," she wrote. "It's time I stopped letting her tell me how to live. Why should I care what she thinks? I have so little time."

She was slightly high, like a person just after the first electric sip of a martini, and she did exactly what she felt like doing. She had always wanted to serve people, and now she simply started helping those around her. She would never be a doctor, but she could care for sick friends, and she often had them stay with her for months on end. She made a kind of family of other people's children and grandchildren, and they were constantly in and out of her house.

She took in student boarders too. She said it was to help pay the rent, but it was really because she liked having young people in the apartment. Her phone was always busy, her apartment always full of life. She traveled — to Russia, to India, to visit old friends in France and Switzerland. And she invited them to visit her.

She filled her life with all the things that she had always wanted — art, music, people — and freed herself from everything that did not make her happy. When she found that Bob and I could not keep from treating her like the sad old Mom she used to be, she simply cut us loose. She did not need that. For the happiest years of her life, Mom relied almost entirely on herself.

She wrote the very last note in the box when she was almost eighty. By then her arthritic hands had trouble grasping the pen, and her handwriting had turned into a hesitant wavering line. But the words are strong, positive, optimistic, without a single uncertain note. "I am not going to lower my sights," Mom wrote. "I am going to live up to the best in myself. Even if it means some painful changes. I am no longer afraid."

GIFTS

That last letter was my mother's final gift to me, and I read it with tears running down my face. She had no way to know that I would ever find it, or how happy I would be to discover that at the end of her life she finally found her truest self. She had traveled through obedience to anger and rebellion and finally come to rest in a place where she was not only independent, but also happy.

Meeting Mom — the real Mom — was even harder than I had expected. I never thought her life was easy, but until I read her letters I had not known the enormous burden of pain that she carried with her. Each letter was like a reproach, and as I thought about the Mim Tales I wished that I had been more considerate, more understanding, that I had given her more support. Mom was so generous to me, and I gave so little in return.

In her own oblique way Mom passed on all the knowledge she had gleaned, giving me the tools I needed not to become her. Believing that work, beauty, marriage and mother-hood were the forces that had shaped her destiny, she tried to teach me how to do better at each of them than she had.

Work was her most basic lesson: Using herself as an example, she made me see that working is as necessary as breathing. Mom's strongest belief was that "it is what we are made for," and she was convinced that those who are not useful can never be satisfied. She tried to make me see that a job was not enough; she wanted me to have the meaningful career that she herself had yearned for.

Stamped at an early age by her own lack of beauty, Mom tried to spare me that pain. The fate of men is not decided by their looks, and my mother did not want beauty — or the lack of it — to determine my destiny. Throughout human history beauty has been seen as a gift from God, but Mom had another notion; she thought that beauty could be earned through self-knowledge. It may be a revolutionary idea, but it has offered me great comfort.

Mom also had her own ideas about marriage. Unlike most women of her time, she did not think that a woman needed a man to be complete. She believed that marriage was important, but she tried to show me that it works only when it is based on mutual respect between two people who encourage each other to live up to the best in themselves.

But Mom's most important lesson was how to be a mother. I see now how hard she tried to be a good one, despite her many handicaps. Her struggle with her own mother had shown her that it is important to encourage your children to be themselves, even if they do not turn out to be the people that you wish they were. And so she urged me to independence, asking only that I work hard, be kind and live up to my own possibilities.

Growing up, I was utterly oblivious to the fact that Mom was teaching me all that. But I was instantly aware of her final lesson, which was hidden in her notes and letters. As I read them I began to understand that in the end you are the only one who can make yourself happy. More important, Mom showed me that it is never too late to find out how to do it.

ACKNOWLEDGMENTS

So many people helped me with this book that I will never be able to thank them all. But here's a start.

Women in Communications: If they had not given me the Matrix Award, I never would have channeled Mom to thank them for it. And if the members had not responded so generously, I never would have tried to turn the speech into a book.

My agent, Kathy Robbins, who spent hours talking me through this project, reading pages, sending encouraging notes.

All of the people who told me stories about their mothers. I don't think there was a single interview that did not end in tears.

My colleagues at *Gourmet* — Doc Willoughby, Larry Karol, Richard Ferretti, Bill Sertl and Robin Pellicci — who pitched in every time I said, "I can't do that because I'm working on the book."

My brother, Bob Half, who has always been the best big brother anyone could ever have.

My guys, Michael and Nick Singer, who are endlessly supportive.

Above all, my editor Ann Godoff, who saw exactly what this book should be even when I did not. She kept saying, "Don't worry, you'll get it right." Great editing is a great gift, and it is one for which I am truly grateful.

And as always, thanks to the Mac-Dowell Colony, where I started working on what eventually turned out to be this book. It is, perhaps, my favorite place on earth.

ABOUT THE AUTHOR

Ruth Reichl is the editor in chief of *Gourmet* magazine and the author of the bestsellers *Tender at the Bone* and *Comfort Me with Apples*. She has been the restaurant critic at the *New York Times* and the food editor at the *Los Angeles Times*.

The employees of Thorndike Press hope you have enjoyed this Large Print book. All our Thorndike, Wheeler, and Kennebec Large Print titles are designed for easy reading, and all our books are made to last. Other Thorndike Press Large Print books are available at your library, through selected bookstores, or directly from us.

For information about titles, please call:
 (800) 223-1244

or visit our Web site at:
 http://gale.cengage.com/thorndike

To share your comments, please write:
 Publisher
 Thorndike Press
 295 Kennedy Memorial Drive
 Waterville, ME 04901